EXTREME ANIMALS

BRILLIANT BIRDS

Isabel Thomas

Raintree

Chicago, Illinois

www.capstonepub.com
Visit our website to find out more information about Heinemann-Raintree books.

To order:

☎ Phone 800-747-4992

🖥 Visit www.capstonepub.com to browse our catalog and order online.

Edited by Daniel Nunn, John-Paul Wilkins, and Rebecca Rissman
Designed by Philippa Jenkins
Picture research by Elizabeth Alexander
Production by Victoria Fitzgerald

Originated by Capstone Global Library
Printed and bound in China by CTPS

16 15 14 13 12
10 9 8 7 6 5 4 3 2 1

Library of Congress Cataloging-in-Publication Data

Cataloging-in-Publication data is on file at the Library of Congress.

ISBN:

978-1-4109-4678-2 (HC) 978-1-4109-4684-3 (PB)

Acknowledgments

We would like to thank the following for permission to reproduce photographs: © Jolyon Troscianko p. 22; Alamy p. 27 (© Frans Lanting Studio); iStockphoto pp. 9 (© Bob Balestri), 15 (© Tobias Müller), 20 (© ChristianWilkinson), 25 (© Patrycja Zboch); Nature Picture Library pp. 8 (© Rolf Nussbaumer), 23 (© Miles Barton); Photolibrary pp. 12 (Antoine Dervaux/Bios), 14 (Michel & Christine Denis-Huot/Bios), 17 (Konrad Wothe/OSF), 21 (Mark Jones/Age footstock), 26 (Mark Carwardine/Peter Arnold Images); Photoshot p. 18 (imagebroker/Ulrich Doering); Shutterstock pp. 4 (© Tom Davison), 5 (© Borislav Borisov), 6 (© Luiz Claudio Ribeiro), 7 (© Graeme Shannon), 10 (© John Carnemolla), 11 (© Roadworks), 13 (© Christian Musat), 16 (© EcoPrint), 19 (© Dmitry_Tsvetkov), 24 (© Vishnevskiy Vasily).

Main cover photograph of pink flamingo reproduced with permission of Shutterstock (© FER737NG). Background cover photograph of feathers reproduced with permission of Shutterstock (© Naomi Hasegawa).

Every effort has been made to contact copyright holders of material reproduced in this book. Any omissions will be rectified in subsequent printings if notice is given to the publisher.

Disclaimer
All the Internet addresses (URLs) given in this book were valid at the time of going to press. However, due to the dynamic nature of the Internet, some addresses may have changed, or sites may have changed or ceased to exist since publication. While the author and publisher regret any inconvenience this may cause readers, no responsibility for any such changes can be accepted by either the author or the publisher.

Some words are shown in bold, **like this**. You can find out what they mean by looking in the glossary.

Contents

Extreme Birds

Do you think you know everything about birds? Think again! All birds have wings and feathers. But the differences between birds can make them **extreme**.

Some birds have bizarre bodies. Some behave in weird ways. These features help them to find **mates** or food—or to avoid getting eaten themselves!

Extreme colors help some male birds to attract female birds.

DID YOU KNOW?

Bee-eaters can remove a bee's stinger before eating the bee!

Regal Eagles

Champion human weight lifters can lift one-and-a-half times their body weight. This is nothing compared to eagle power. Some eagles can carry monkeys or deer four times their weight!

DID YOU KNOW?
Eagles attack and eat anything they can carry, including snakes!

huge eyes to spot **prey**

sharp **talons**

7

Helicopter Hummingbirds

How long would it take you to flap your arms 90 times? Some hummingbirds can flap their wings 90 times in one second! This helps them to **hover** in front of flowers.

DID YOU KNOW?
Hummingbirds need lots of energy. They eat every 10 minutes and visit up to 1,500 flowers every day.

long beak for reaching **nectar** inside flowers

Bee hummingbirds are just over 2 inches long. That is smaller than many rain forest butterflies!
actual size

Outsized Ostriches

Ostriches are the world's biggest birds. They are too heavy to fly, but they don't need to. They can run at more than 40 miles per hour. That is fast enough to escape most **predators**. Each stride can be as long as two cars!

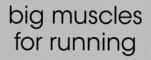

big muscles for running

world's largest eggs

11

Tough Penguins

Emperor penguins survive the world's worst weather in the **Antarctic**. Icy **blizzards** make it feel three times colder than a freezer! Each male spends the winter looking after an egg. If a penguin drops its egg, the chick inside will freeze to death in two minutes.

Male Emperor penguins huddle together to keep warm in the freezing cold.

DID YOU KNOW?

Penguins have spiky tongues. This helps the birds to grip slippery fish.

Revolting Vultures

When **predators** like lions kill an animal, they leave the most disgusting parts behind. Vultures find this rotting meat and gobble it up! They eat so much that it becomes difficult for them to fly.

DID YOU KNOW?
Egyptian vultures use rocks to break open ostrich eggs.

15

Bird Builders and Artists

Weaver birds build the world's largest nests. The nests are like large apartment buildings, with room for hundreds of birds. Living together protects the birds from **predators**.

nest

Male bowerbirds are artists. They make beautiful displays with flowers, leaves, and other pretty things. They want to impress female bowerbirds.

plastic spoon

feathers

bottle cap

17

Fearless Flamingos

This lake is hot, stinky, and poisonous. The water would kill most animals. But flamingos can feed safely here. They have special **bills** that **filter** food from the water.

A flock of flamingos can contain up to one million birds.

DID YOU KNOW?
The bend in a flamingo's leg is actually its ankle.

ankle

19

Soaring Albatrosses

Albatrosses hunt, eat, and sleep at sea. Some don't set foot on land for 10 years at a time.

An albatross can fly for days without flapping its huge wings. It uses energy from wind to stay in the air.

21

Clever Crows

Crows are very clever. They think like humans! They are the only birds that can invent new tools. They make hooks from sticks and leaves. They use their tools to scoop insects from small holes.

DID YOU KNOW?

Some crows have figured out a way to crack walnuts. They wait next to a busy road. When the traffic stops, they hop out and put the walnuts on the road. Cars drive over the nuts and break them open.

Tongue - Twisting Woodpeckers

Imagine that your tongue reached your knees! A woodpecker's tongue is two-thirds the length of its body. It uses its tongue to grab food from holes in trees. The tip of its tongue can sense **vibrations** made by moving insects.

DID YOU KNOW?

The woodpecker's tongue is like a tape measure. When the tongue is not being used, it coils around the woodpecker's skull inside its head.

Noisy Kakapos

Kakapos are the fattest parrots in the world. Males make a booming sound to attract females. The noise can be heard up to 3 miles away!

The male kakapo sucks in air until he is as big as a soccer ball. Then he releases a deep boom. He does this every night for two or three months!

Record-Breakers

Which bird do you think is the most **extreme**? Why? Take a look at some of these record-breaking birds to help you decide.

What? Common swift

Why? Longest flight without stopping

Wow! When swifts leave their nests for the first time, they fly non-stop for two years. They can travel 310,000 miles in one trip. That is farther away than the Moon!

What? Ruppell's vulture

Why? Highest flying bird

Wow! This high flyer has been spotted at a height of 37,000 feet. That is high enough to peer into the windows of a jumbo jet!

What? Albatross

Why? Longest wings

Wow! The wings of the wandering albatross are over 11 feet from tip to tip. That is like 17 soccer balls in a row!

What? Peregrine falcon

Why? Fastest flying bird

Wow! When chasing **prey**, Peregrine falcons dive-bomb as fast as 155 miles per hour!

What? Ostrich

Why? Largest bird's egg

Wow! One ostrich egg can weigh as much as 24 chicken eggs!

What? Kakapo

Why? Longest-living bird

Wow! No bird has more birthdays than a kakapo. These parrots can live for more than 100 years!

29

Glossary

Antarctic land or seas at or near the South Pole

bill hard mouth part of a bird or other animal

blizzard long, heavy snowstorm

extreme unusual, amazing, or different from normal

filter remove or separate from liquid

hover stay hanging in the air

mate animal that can have babies with another animal

nectar sweet, sugary liquid made by flowers

predator animal that hunts other animals for food

prey animal that is hunted by another animal for food

tagged fitted with a tiny radio that tells scientists where the animal is

talon claw of an eagle or other bird of prey

vibration small back and forth movement that makes a noise

Find Out More

Books

Berger, Melvin, and Gilda Berger. *Birds* (True or False). New York: Scholastic, 2010.

Huggins-Cooper, Lynne. *Beastly Birds and Bats* (Awesome Animals). Mankato, Minn.: QEB, 2008.

Solway, Andrew. *Birds of Prey* (Wild Predators). Chicago: Heinemann Library, 2005.

Web sites

Learn more about birds and animals of all kinds at this National Geographic web site:
animals.nationalgeographic.com/animals/birds

Help to protect bald eagles, the national symbol of the United States:
www.eagles.org

This web site of the Smithsonian National Zoo includes fact sheets, games, and more about birds:
nationalzoo.si.edu/animals/birds/forkids/default.cfm

31

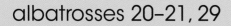